Do It All Again!

LEANNA POLAND

Written by Leanna Poland

ISBN: 0998545503
ISBN 13: 9780998545509
Library of Congress Control Number: 2016921561
Color Your Soul Mininstries, Denver, COLORADO

DEDICATION

*This book is dedicated to everyone who
needs the courage to begin again.*

BEGIN AGAIN...

"Just pick yourself up and start again."

I f you're reading this that means you're still alive, and you should know it's never too late to start over. Life is like a puzzle. Simply pick-up the pieces and start putting them together. Slowly but surely they will begin to take shape and form a picture - a picture of your life. Sure, mistakes have been made. Perhaps tragedy has struck and things have fallen apart, but life goes on. How it goes, depends on you. Learn from your mistakes, let go of the past and grasp the future. There is a wonderful one waiting for you! Take control of your own life and move forward. Tomorrow brings a new day and with it new opportunities. Step into the future, take it one day at a time and start again. It's never too late to build the life you want or to become the person you want to be. The only thing holding you back is you.

> *"...forgetting those things that are behind and reaching forward to those things which are ahead, I press toward the goal for the prize of the upward call of God in Christ Jesus."*

(Phil. 3:13-14)

DREAM AGAIN...

"Never give up on your dreams.
Never. Never. Never."

Dreams, we all have them. Now I'm not talking about the kind of dreams you have while you're sleeping. I'm talking about the dreams that take hold of your spirit and refuse to let go. It could be a dream placed in your heart by the Lord that makes you stretch, reach and operate outside of your comfort zone. A dream of significance for you and for others designed for a purpose. Remember that kind of dream? What is your dream? Has it slipped through your fingers? Then grasp hold of it again and work to turn your dream into a reality and pursue it with all of your heart. Dreams are what we do when we're awake, not while we sleep. Walt Disney once said, "If you can dream it, you can do it." Keep following your dreams. Don't stop until you accomplish them and remember that dreamers can change the world.

"Therefore, my beloved brethren, be stead-
fast, immovable, always abounding in
the work of the Lord, knowing that your
labor is not in vain in the Lord."

(1 Cor. 15:58)

REACH AGAIN...

*"Just when you think you can't
reach any higher; stretch."*

You will never grow or get beyond where you are if you don't strive for more. Settling is simply not an option. Choose things that are out of your comfort zone. Read books that are harder to understand. Hang out with people who are smarter than you, people who make you stretch to keep up with them. Study a different language. Take some classes and acquire new skills. Get out from in front of the T.V. and expand your horizons. Travel and see new places, meet new people and learn about the world in which you live. Don't settle for the status quo. Set yourself goals, use mile-markers and put things into action one step at a time. Les Brown once said, "Shoot for the moon. Even if you miss, you'll land among the stars." Reach…then reach some more. Never, ever stop reaching.

"Not that I have already attained, or
am already perfected; but I press on,
that I may lay hold of that for which
Christ Jesus has also laid hold of me."

(Phil. 3:12)

BELIEVE AGAIN...

"Christianity is a lens to the world.
By it, everything comes into focus."

If you look at the world through the eyes of Christianity, or through the eyes of Christ, you will come to understand the world in a way that you have never understood it before. But you must come with an open mind and open spirit. You might not believe at first. You may struggle, fight and even deny. But if you pray, and ask God to help you understand, He will not let you down. You will come to discover, the same way many people have, that the world you live in makes more sense when you see it through the eyes of Christ and through Christianity. After all, God created the world, and no one knows how it works better than He does. Take a chance on Him. You won't be sorry that you did.

"...Believe in the Lord your God,
and you shall be established..."

(2 Chr. 20:20)

TRUST AGAIN...

"Be careful where you place your trust."

Every day people fail us, society fails us, the government and the economy fails us. If you put all of your faith in the things of this world you will inevitably be disappointed. Your husband may leave you, your IRA might disappear when the economy takes a dive, and that "secure" job you had for years could vanish when your company gets bought out. When we place all of our faith and trust in worldly items, we are in for disappointment. So place your faith in something that can't be lost and will never fade - eternal life through Jesus Christ. Jim Elliot once said, "He is no fool who gives up what he cannot keep to gain what he cannot lose." Jesus promises to never leave or forsake us, no matter what happens in our lives. So give up seeking after things that can be lost and instead grab hold of what you can never lose.

> *"Some trust in chariots, and some*
> *in horses; But we will remember the*
> *name of the Lord our God."*

> *(Ps. 20:7)*

SHINE AGAIN...

"Surprise someone, or even yourself;
do something out of the ordinary."

When is the last time you tried something new or unpredictable? Maybe you sang a song, or danced with your friends at a party. Perhaps you painted your bedroom daffodil yellow or your living room sage green. You might have quit your job and started your own business. Maybe you published a book, and no one even knew you could write, or you learned to play the piano and gave a "mini" concert for you family at Christmas. Possibly, you stepped way out of your comfort zone and bought a red dress, red shoes and long dangling earrings and blew them away at the wedding! When was the last time you dazzled them? Try it... they need it and so do you!

> *"...It is good and fitting for one to eat and drink, and to enjoy the good of all his labor in which he toils under the sun all the days of his life which God gives him; for it is his heritage."*
>
> *(Eccl. 5:18)*

TRY AGAIN....

*"A person will never reach their full
potential if they refuse to try."*

Try, and if you fail, try again. If you never try you will never know what you are capable of doing. Helen Keller was blind, yet that never stopped her. She was the first deaf-blind person to earn a Bachelor of Arts degree and became a world-famous speaker and author. She once said, "We can do anything we want, as long as we stick to it long enough." Winston Churchill had a speech impediment, but went on to become one of the most inspiring speakers of modern times, and even won a Nobel Peace prize. Most people have no idea how many times Abraham Lincoln failed at business, or at senate and congressional races before he became one of America's greatest Presidents. So be persistent and keep on trying. You will amaze yourself at what you can do.

"…let us run with endurance the
race that is set before us…"

(Heb. 12:1)

INSPIRE AGAIN

"Inspiration often comes from discontentment."

When people are discontent, one of two things happens - they give up on life or decide to make a change.

Florence Nightingale was a person who chose change. When she saw the deplorable conditions that wounded soldiers lived in during the Crimean war, she set about to make changes; and what changes she made! She campaigned for reforms in hospitals and medical facilities. She started schools to train nurses, and helped make nursing the respectable field it is today. She encouraged doctors, hospital directors, and even politicians to get involved. This led to safer, more efficient hospitals and medical facilities. She dedicated her entire life to improving the field of medicine and inspired others to do the same. Discontent with something you see in the world? Then get inspired to change it, and motivate others to get involved.

"...stir up the gift of God which is in you..."

(2 Tim. 1:6)

LOVE AGAIN...

*"Jesus built an empire - not
by force but by love."*

Leaders throughout history have built their empires on the backs of conquered people. They subdued nation after nation through war and by force. But Jesus Christ came along, and showed people a different way of building an empire. He used love. Love means showing a person a better way to live, and giving them the freedom to make the choice of accepting or rejecting the offer. True love is never forcing someone to do what you want. Love conquers by patience, generosity, graciousness and truth. Love changes hearts. Jesus did with love, what no military leader has ever been able to do. He gained the loyalty, respect, dedication and love of the people He encountered.

> *"Now abide faith, hope, love, these*
> *three; but the greatest of these is love."*
>
> *(1 Cor. 13:13)*

HELP AGAIN...

"Moments we remember: When we helped others."

When is the last time you lent a helping hand to someone in need? Not because you wanted the world to know. Not to receive praise or a pat on the back, but because it was the right thing to do, and you truly wanted to help. You saw a need and your compassion led you to fulfill it. Jesus spent His time on earth meeting the needs of others. He healed the sick, fed the hungry, and raised the dead, just to name a few. Even when He was tired and exhausted, He never turned away anyone in need. We can't take care of everyone, or support every organization, but the majority of us could help out a lot more than we do. Reach out and help when you get the chance, because someone out there needs it.

"Give to him who asks you, and from him who wants to borrow from you do not turn away."

(Matt. 5:42)

LAUGH AGAIN...

"Both the body and soul need laughter."

When is the last time you had a good laugh? Not at someone else's expense but just a good old fashioned laugh! Maybe it was a funny movie, a great joke or something one of the kids said. Maybe you did something that made you laugh at yourself. We could all use more laughter in our lives. Children are great at laughing, they laugh about everything! They don't even need a reason. Adults are way too serious. We should make a point to laugh more. Doctor's claim laughter helps to heal the physical body, allowing us to live longer. Dr. Madan Kataria once said, "I have not seen anyone dying of laughter, but I know millions who are dying because they are not laughing." Laughter relieves stress, mends the soul and lifts the spirit. So laugh more this week. You will be glad that you did!

> *"To everything there is a season...a time to laugh."*
>
> *(Ecc. 3:1, 4)*

PRAY AGAIN...

"Sometimes, down on your knees
is the only place left to go."

Prayer changes things. Some people don't believe it but it does. Prayer connects us with the Creator of the universe. It opens the lines of communication between heaven and earth. Prayer gives God the chance to work on our behalf and to provide for our needs. He sends people to help during a time of crisis, provides the perfect job at the right moment, and heals our mind and bodies. Prayer puts things into motion. I'm not sure why we make it our last resort, instead of our first. Furthermore, God tells us that He hears all of our prayers, and that not one of them goes unheeded. He watches out for our well-being. God cares for us, and we should take everything to Him in prayer.

> *"Be anxious for nothing, but in everything by prayer and supplication, with thanksgiving, let your requests be made known to God..."*
>
> *(Phil. 4:6)*

EXERCISE AGAIN...

"Exercise: It takes discipline and a lot of whining!"

I'd rather not exercise. I'd rather sit on the couch and read a book. I'd rather eat ice cream than fruit. I'd rather eat steak than salmon. But I know I have to exercise to keep my joints moving (especially at my age), and eat healthier foods if I want to stay healthy. But it's not easy to do. It takes dedication. So what about you - have your exercised lately? If you haven't, then get started. Take a walk around the block, go for a swim, or learn to jog, play a sport, or join an exercise class. Exercise helps to keep your weight under control, your joints limber, and helps you to live longer. It relieves stress, and lifts your spirit. It helps keep you mentally alert, and more focused. "Use it or lose it," the saying goes. If you don't want to lose your good health, then get moving before it disappears.

"But I discipline my body and
bring it into subjection…"

(1 Cor. 9:27)

THINK AGAIN...

*"Check out the things you are being told.
Don't accept everything as truth."*

God created humans giving them brains capable of incredible creativity and thinking. Unfortunately we tend to let the news media, politicians, and even some preachers do all of our thinking for us. It's time to stop. Use the incredible mind the Lord gave you, and start doing your own thinking. Don't believe every story you see on the Internet or T.V. Check out the sources they are using. The same holds true for Biblical teaching. Just because someone claims to be a Christian, doesn't mean they are preaching the truth. Early followers of the apostle Paul compared his teaching with the Old Testament scriptures to make sure Paul was preaching the truth. We should do no less. After all, that's why the Lord blessed us with brains.

"Get wisdom! Get understanding..."

(Prov. 4:5)

CHOOSE AGAIN...

"Our future depends on the choices we make."

God gave mankind "free will" empowering us with the ability to make our own choices. Our days are filled with decisions that we have to make. Some turn out good, others not so much. But of all the decisions we have to make, none is as important as the choice we make about our salvation. We have the choice to accept or reject Jesus Christ as our Savior. Our destiny lies with that choice. If we follow the ways of the world, our fate will be quite different than if we follow the Lord. Act on the Lord's offer, and avoid the outcome that awaits if you don't make that choice. But you must choose. Either you are with the Lord or you are against Him. Either you are saved or you aren't.

> "...choose for yourselves this day whom
> you will serve...But as for me and my
> house, we will serve the Lord."

> (Josh. 24:15)

LOOK AGAIN...

*"Make sure the Lord is the
first thing on your list."*

When is the last time you stopped and took inventory of your priorities in life? What is it that you really worship the most? Is it money and all the things it can buy? Maybe it's your job and climbing the corporate ladder. How about your beauty and the determination to stay young, or importance placed on closets full of clothes? Is there a certain man or woman in your life that you're constantly trying to please? God's first Commandment tells us we should have no other God's before Him. He is to be number "One". When we become obsessed with something, it can become a "god" in our lives. When we spend all of our time trying to obtain it, maintain it, and save it, it has replaced God and become an "idol" we worship. Take a look at your life this week, and see if you need to adjust your priorities. Take a look at what you really worship.

> *"And I am the Lord your God... "You*
> *shall have no other gods before Me."*
>
> *(Ex. 20:2-3)*

REST AGAIN...

A little R & R goes a long ways toward recovery."

When is the last time you had a little rest and relaxation? I don't mean, a "plop down" on the couch with a bag of chips and a cold drink in your hand. I'm talking about quality time relaxing and resting from the hustle and bustle of life. The Bible tells us that God did all His creating in six days, and then rested on the seventh. God didn't create a day of rest because He needed it. He created it because He knew man would need it. We wear ourselves out both mentally and physically when we don't take some time to re-charge. Learn to take one day out of the week for a little rest and relaxation. Not only will you enjoy it and feel better, but the people around you will notice a difference too. Go fishing or take a scenic ride on your bike. Grab a book and spend the day sitting by the ocean, or relaxing in your hammock. Revive with a little R & R!

> *"Come to Me, all you who labor and are*
> *heavy laden, and I will give you rest."*
>
> *(Matt. 11:28)*

CREATE AGAIN...

"Creativity is seeing what others don't see."

Our God is a creative God. He said, "Let there be…" and there it was. When is the last time you said, "Let there be," and created something? Being creative means taking your ideas and bringing them to life. Where would the world be if people never used their creativity? The source of every human invention, every work of art and every idea, came forth because someone used their creative skills. We can have a tremendous impact on the world around us when we utilize the artistic gifts and talents God has blessed us with. He expects us to enrich the world around us, not hoard, hide or bury our creative talents. Take that idea that has been spinning around in your head for days, months or years, and make it a reality! Someone needs to benefit from your ingenious talent!

"In the beginning God created…"

(Gen. 1:1)

DARE AGAIN...

"Take a chance. The out-
come may surprise you."

Her name was Isak Denison. One day she packed her bags and headed off to Africa. There she bought a farm and started a coffee plantation. In Africa she traveled, helping the natives, and daring to do things most *men* would never do. Eventually the farm failed, she went broke and had to return to Denmark. But after returning, she decided to record her adventures. The result: a bestselling book called "Out of Africa". She went on to become an outstanding author. Had she not dared to go to Africa, she never would have written her book. We can go through our whole lives being afraid to step out and try something new. But when we finally get the courage, life responds in an amazing way. Take some chances in your own life. Step out and do something daring. The results may not be what you planned, but even better!

"...be of good courage, and do it."

(Ezra 10:4)

APPRECIATE AGAIN...

"Everyone is unique but we often don't appreciate it."

God created each one of us to be distinct, different, diverse individuals. Yet the world constantly resets the "specifications", the terms, the things required of us before we fit in. Sometimes we feel like "misfits." Cast aside because we have flaws and imperfections, we set out to change everything about ourselves in the hope of being accepted. Inevitably we end-up wasting precious time and resources. The Bible tells us that God "knit" us together. Do you have any idea how long it takes to knit something? It takes a great deal of time, along with great care and precision. We insult our God when we criticize ourselves. So just stop, and instead learn to appreciate the fact that there is no one else in the world exactly like you!

"For you formed my inward parts; you knitted me together in my mother's womb."

(Ps. 139:13)
(ESV)

SIMPLIFY AGAIN...

*"Clutter helps you avoid what is truly
going on in your inner world."*

For over twenty years I have done professional decorating, merchandising, and organizing, and I can say this with truth and confidence: If your outside world is disorganized and cluttered, there is something going on in your inner world. There is a reason for all that clutter. Figure out why and start simplifying your outer world. Clean out, throw out, and re-organize. Once you do, you'll find you have extra time on your hands. Scary right? Why? Because when you're not shuffling through the clutter, you have more time to examine your inner world. In fact, fear of change is what often keeps people from organizing their outer world. Clutter hides the real problem. Be brave. Organize your outer world. When you do, you will be surprised at your own personal growth.

> *"Do not lay up for yourselves treasures on earth…but lay up for yourselves treasures in heaven…"*

> *(Matt. 6:19)*

COUNT AGAIN...

"Remember; there is always a price to be paid."

People are great at starting things, but finishing them is the problem. They start taking dance lessons, piano lessons, or a painting class. They begin a new diet, join a fitness class, or enroll in college only to drop out. People tend to be quitters. Why? They don't count the cost before they begin. People say to themselves, "Oh, I can do that." But before they start they don't consider the time, energy, money, or commitment it takes to see it through. They step out and begin but soon discover it's much more difficult than they had planned. It's easier to quit, than to put forth the effort and time it takes to learn or finish something. Even Jesus tells us to weigh the cost before we choose to follow Him. Decide what it is you want to do and decide if you're willing to pay the cost before you start.

"For which of you, intending to build a tower, does not sit down first and count the cost, whether he has enough to finish it…"

(Luke 14:28)

REFUSE AGAIN...

"Don't allow the negative voices around you to penetrate your spirit."

Elizabeth the 1st of England refused to be swayed by the men that surrounded her. They told her she needed to marry, that a woman could not rule England, and she would never survive. Surprise! She showed them. She wasn't about to settle for second place behind a King. She ruled England for eighteen years, and her reign was called the "Golden Age" of England because of the peace, and prosperity it brought to the nation. Elizabeth refused to settle for anything other than being "the ruling" Queen. Learn not to settle in life. Don't settle for a job you hate, a relationship that is abusive, or what other people say is best for you. Take charge of you own life and create your own destiny. Refuse to accept what you really don't want. Instead, follow your heart.

"Whoever has no rule over his own spirit,
is like a city broken down, without walls."

(Prov. 25:28)

HOPE AGAIN...

*"A hope of "everlasting" life awaits
all those that believe in Jesus."*

The sun always rises in the morning, just as it always sets in the evening. But there are times in our lives when things seem so black and bleak we wonder if the sun will really rise. What pushes us on and gets us up the next morning to see if the sun has risen? How about hope? Hope keeps us moving forward. Not the kind of hope that the world has to offer, the hope of more money, or fame, material possessions or to find the perfect relationship. These are all temporary things. It's the "lasting hope" provided by the Lord that keeps us moving on. The kind of hope that Job had, that there is a God in heaven, that He is alive and has everything under control. Through Him we have eternal salvation, and one day He will stand upon the earth again in the flesh (Job 19:25-27). Do you know any other thing you hope for that is guaranteed? Then hope in the Lord.

> *"This hope we have as an anchor of the*
> *soul, both sure and steadfast..."*
>
> *(Heb. 6:19)*

SEE AGAIN...

*"The only way to see the world is
to take the time to look."*

See Dick and Jane. See Spot run. See the snow on the mountain peaks. See the ocean waves. See the children playing. See the yellow daffodils. See the pink cherry blossoms. See the roses in your back yard. See the church steeple. See your children grow. See someone in need. See the birds building their nest. See the workers in the field. See the choir singing. See the children laughing. See the sunset. See the sunrise. See the majestic clouds in the sky. See the kayakers in the river. See the fisherman. See the artwork on the wall. See the whales. See the dolphins. See the wedding party. See the cupcakes in the window. See the hotdog vender. See the people leaving church. See the dancers. See the fields of sunflowers. See the wheat blowing in the wind. See the world around you, and see it every day. Because once this day is over, it will never come again.

> *"Come and see the works of God; He is awesome in His doing toward the sons of men."*
>
> *(Ps. 66:5)*

ENJOY AGAIN...

"If you haven't been enjoying your life lately, then now is the time to begin."

We tell ourselves *someday* we will enjoy life. Someday, after we accomplish everything that we want to accomplish. Problem being, there is always something else to strive for: A bigger house, a better job, a little more money, a new car, that perfect vacation. We're always so busy reaching for more, that we don't take the time to enjoy what we have at the moment. Before we know it, half of life has passed us by. Learn to live in the moment. Enjoy what you are doing and take in your surroundings. If you're planting your garden, enjoy the scent of the flowers, the birds singing and the sun shining. Soak in all the beauty that is around you, and learn to make the moment enjoyable. You only pass this way once.

"This is the day the Lord has made;
We will rejoice and be glad in it."

(Ps. 118:24)

SING AGAIN...

"Don't just sing in the shower; sing everywhere."

I admire people that have great voices because I for one can't carry a tune. Music is such an uplifting thing for the soul because it gets the spirit moving in a positive direction. I love to sing along when a great song is playing. I crank up the volume, (so no one can hear my voice), and go for it. I love that music connects people of all ages and nationalities. Even if you can't understand the words, you can enjoy the music. I believe God has filled heaven and earth with musical notes, and that they are floating around, waiting for some great artist to grasp them, write them down on paper, and make a beautiful song. Find the kind of music you like, play it, sing along, and fill heaven and earth with it! Don't worry about the fact that you can't carry a tune. Just sing and have some fun! Besides, most of the people singing along with you can't carry a tune either!

"Oh, sing to the Lord a new song!
Sing to the Lord, all the earth.

(Ps. 96:1)

SAIL AGAIN...

"You can't see much from the shoreline."

If your boat has been tied to the dock for the majority of your life, you don't know what you're missing. It's only when you untie the boat and "set sail", that you discover new worlds. But you'll never untie the boat if your heart is full of fear. It takes courage and faith to launch the boat and face the unknown. Amy Carmichael did just that. She left her home in Ireland to become a missionary to India. She opened an orphanage and founded a mission in Dohnavur. While there she saved hundreds of children from being sold to the Buddhist temples for the purpose of prostitution (India outlawed temple prostitution in 1948). Her facility still helps children to this day in India. Think of all the saved lives because she "untied" her boat from Ireland and set sail. Sail your vessel. Take some chances and dare to steer into uncharted waters. You will never know what you are missing until you do.

"Launch out into the deep..."

(Luke 5:4)

IMAGINE AGAIN...

*"Imagination is a gift from God, so
use it to the best of your ability."*

Imagination brings new products, new ideas, and new ways of doing things to the world. Everything we see, every creation, began in someone's imagination. Someone imagined a rocket to the moon, and created one. Henry Ford imagined an automobile that middle class Americans could afford and built one. Michelangelo examined a piece of marble and created a statue of David. Walt Disney visualized a play world for children and Disneyland came into being. Thomas Edison imagined hearing his own voice, and invented the phonograph. He imagined a cheaper and better light bulb, then created one. Alexander Graham Bell invented the telephone after inventing a device that drew vibrations from the human voice to help deaf people visualize sound. All these people dared to imagine and then went to work. Imagination is a powerful thing.

"Every good gift and perfect gift is from above..."

(James 1:17)

ELIMINATE AGAIN...

"Habits change when we change."

Bad habits are hard to break. There's nothing easy about quitting smoking or drinking. It's not easy to stop overeating, to quit hoarding or to stop procrastinating. But as Desiderius Erasmus once said, "Habit is overcome by habit." If you want to replace a bad habit in your life, then learn to replace it with something better. Replace overeating with exercise or watching too much T.V. with reading. Replace drinking with meetings at A.A. or join a support group. Seek some counseling if you can't stop shopping. We often develop habits because we have something going on inside of us that we refuse to deal with. Do some soul searching, and be honest with what you find. Correct the problem on the inside and the habit will be easier to change. We can change our habits.

"The end of a thing is better than its beginning..."

(Eccl. 7:8)

GIVE-UP AGAIN...

*"The only person you can change
in a relationship is you."*

If you have a plan to try and change someone else, give it up. It will never work, because YOU are the one that needs to change. You have to alter the way you respond to the other person. I heard a story about a man whose wife was always running late. Because he always waited for her, they were late everywhere they went. One summer they had planned a trip to Europe. He told her if she wasn't ready to leave for the airport on time that he would leave without her. She wasn't and he did. She missed the plane, and he flew to Europe by himself. She had to make new arrangements. But guess what? She was never late again. Why? He changed the way he responded to her bad habit. Change yourself! Don't waste your time and energy trying to change others. It will only drive you crazy!

"And why do you look at the speck in your brother's eye, but do not consider the plank in your own eye?"

(Matt. 7:3)

WORK AGAIN...

"Spend your life working at a job you love."

If you're not utilizing your talents in the work that you do, my guess is that you probably don't enjoy your job. God gives everyone certain talents so that we can make a living, contribute to society, and add value to the world around us. People spend a huge portion of their lives at work, and nothing is more miserable than spending it in a job you hate. Yes, it takes time to develop our talents and it doesn't happen overnight. In the meantime, you may have to take a job you dislike so you can pay the bills and support your family. But start figuring out what your talents are. (Most people have more than one.) Decide what it is that you would love to do for the majority of your life, and set some goals to achieve that desire. If you do, you will be happier, and so will the people around you.

"The labor of the righteous leads to life..."

(Prov. 10:16)

WITHHOLD AGAIN...

"I've learned as I've gotten older; I don't always need to speak my mind."

Withholding one's tongue isn't easy, which is probably why the Bible has a great deal to say about it and the problems it causes. It likens the tongue to fire; the things that roll off of it can burn to the soul. Once spoken, words can never be taken back again. That's why it's so important to beware of the words that leave our mouths. The words that leave our mouths should be uplifting and kind. Our words should always leave others feeling good and glad that we are a part of their lives. Besides, Jesus said, "That out of the abundance of the heart the mouth speaks" (Matt. 12:34). In other words, what we are really harboring in our hearts comes out of our mouths. It's really not a mouth problem; it's a heart problem. Clean up the heart and the mouth will follow.

> *"Let no corrupt word proceed out of your mouth, but what is good for necessary edification, that it may impart grace to the hearer."*
>
> *(Eph. 4:29)*

SMILE AGAIN...

"Smiles are like sunshine - they just brighten your day."

A smile can do amazing things. It can change a person's disposition in an instant. We often forget just how powerful a smile can be. A smile sends a message. It tells others that they have value. When you take the time to smile at someone, it lifts their spirits, and often they smile in return. (After all, you thought they were worth smiling at, so they decided you were worth smiling at too!) Of course we all have bad days. Those days when we're feeling sad or depressed, and a permanent frown has fixed itself to our face. But when someone takes the time to acknowledge us with a smile, we tend to lighten up. Next thing you know, we're passing along smiles to others. Smiles are something everyone needs, so take some time this week to pass some along. It will not only do wonders for others, it will do wonders for you as well!

"...put on tender mercies, kindness..."

(Col. 3:12)

STAND AGAIN...

*"Taking a stand for what's right
is never an easy thing to do."*

William Wilberforce was a member of the British Parliament, and a strong Christian. For twenty years he led a campaign in the British Parliament to end slavery. Slavery put a great deal of money in the pockets of members of Parliament, and they fought tooth and nail to stop the abolition of the slave trade. Time and time again they voted against Wilberforce's bill to end it. He couldn't understand how men of such high rank and power could refuse to do what was right. But he never gave up the fight. In 1807 the Slave Trade Act was passed abolishing the slave trade in the British Empire. It didn't end slavery, but stopped the trade. However, Wilberforce pushed on. Three days before his death in 1833, slavery was abolished throughout the entire British Empire. He took a stand for what was right and never backed down.

> *"Who will rise up for me against the evildoers? Who will stand up for me against the workers of iniquity?"*
>
> *(Ps. 94:16)*

LISTEN AGAIN...

"It's hard to actually listen to someone when you are doing something else at the same time."

Listening is an art, and one that everyone should learn. You will always learn more from listening than you ever will from speaking. To listen means to show that you care, that you value the other person and respect them. It's sad when someone who needs a listening ear can't find one because the other person is texting, checking their email or always answering their phone. It's not only rude, but it's very disrespectful. You can't multitask and listen at the same time. So put your phone away, or at the very least turn down the volume. Send a message that says, "I'm here for you and you have my complete attention" and then give it to them. The day will come when you're the one that needs the listening ear, so take the time to listen to others.

"But whoever listens to me will dwell safely…"

(Prov. 1:33)

OVERCOME AGAIN...

*"To succeed in life, you must
learn to overcome."*

The difference between people that succeed and those that fail is that the people who make it never give up. They look for ways to overcome the obstacles in their path. Singer Julio Iglesias was such a person. At the age of twenty he was involved in a car accident that injured his legs. But he insisted that he would not spend his life in a wheel chair. Little by little he began to move his body. It took him two months just to move his little toe. Two years later, he could walk, but his legs required therapy for several more years. While in the hospital, a nurse gave him a guitar to help pass the time. Soon, he discovered that he had a talent for music. He later became a Grammy award-winning singer. Thank the Lord, most people don't have such a serious obstacle to overcome in their lifetime. But life is filled with problems, and the people that never give up are the ones who grow in success, talent and knowledge. Be an overcomer.

"Do not be overcome by evil, but overcome evil with good."

(Rom. 12:21)

ACCEPT AGAIN...

*"People refuse to accept the fact that they
are responsible for their own lives."*

Some people blame their parents, their siblings, their boss, the government, their first grade teacher, anyone and everyone when life has not turned out the way they wanted. They reason that successful, happy people got that way because they "got all the breaks." And they never got any. Right? Wrong! Success doesn't come from "luck" it comes from hard work. Gary Player once said, "The harder you work, the luckier you get." If there are things you want out of life, accept the fact that you are going to have to earn them. Quit making excuses for not living the life you want and go out and get it. Do whatever it takes. Learn new skills, work longer, learn to save and stop overspending. Set some goals, get off the self-pity bandwagon, and create your own "breaks" in life!

> *"He who has a slack hand becomes poor,*
> *But the hand of the diligent makes rich."*

> *(Prov. 10:4)*

READ AGAIN...

"Everyone should find the time to read."

Read a good book lately? If you haven't, you should. A good book does amazing things. It takes you to faraway lands, teaches, informs, entertains, and educates. You get to travel to and never leave home. Books show us that there is a whole world just waiting to be seen and enjoyed. It's a cheap way to travel. Also, its been shown that children who are read to tend to do better in school and be more adventurous. Sir Richard Steele once said, "Reading is to the mind what exercise is to the body." It helps the muscle of the brain grow stronger, and stay sharper. So... if you haven't picked up a good book lately, do it. It will develop your mind, grow your spirit, enrich your life and expand your horizons.

"Till I come, give attention to reading, to exhortation, to doctrine."

(1Tim. 4:13)

STOP AGAIN...

"If you hurry, you might arrive first, but think about what you missed along the way."

Americans are always in a hurry. We want our computers to immediately fire-up, we can't stand the thirty seconds it takes to get them up and running. We buy our meals at fast food restaurants so we can eat while we drive and save some time. We rush to airports, to meetings, to our children's sports events. We send text messages, because we have no time for a real conversation. The roses are pretty, but who has time to stop and smell them. The sunset is beautiful but who has fifteen minutes just to sit and enjoy it. Sometimes we're in such a hurry that we don't even notice our surroundings. Our minds aren't on the moment, but on where we need to be next. We often forget that life is a journey, and we only get to take it once. Learn to slow down, scale down if you need to, and enjoy your life. When we slow down, we gain inner peace, and a sense of what life is really about.

> *"And let the peace of God*
> *rule in your hearts…"*

> *(Col. 3:15)*

FORGIVE AGAIN...

"Forgiveness should produce forgiveness."

Someone once said that if God had not forgiven us, then heaven would be empty. How very true that statement is. Without God's forgiveness, no one would ever enter heaven. In fact, God was so willing to forgive us, He let His son Jesus Christ die for our sins so we could receive eternal life. If God went to such lengths to forgive us, shouldn't we be willing to forgive others? Surely, there have been times in each of our lives when someone has forgiven us? Besides, failure to forgive steals our inner peace and holds us in bondage. Grudges and anger hurt us more than the person we refuse to forgive. Forgiveness doesn't excuse someone's bad behavior. If it continues, then maybe it's time to move on. However, if the relationship is important, then learn to set some boundaries. We're all human, we all make mistakes, and we all deserve forgiveness.

"For if you forgive men their trespasses, your heavenly Father will also forgive you. But if you do not forgive men their trespasses, neither will your Father forgive your trespasses."

(Matt. 6:14)

AIM AGAIN...

"The only way to aim higher, is to look up."

If your only aim in this life is to get what you can out of it and then die, you need to start aiming higher. This life is temporary. The life you should be aiming for is called "eternal life." It is life beyond what this one has to offer. The world offers temporary satisfaction. Have you ever noticed that as soon as you attain some item for which you were striving that the newness soon wears off, and you start longing for something new? Know why? Material things can never satisfy the inner spirit. Keep trying to fill your inner spirit with anything other than the Lord, and you will have to keep reaching for more. It's like pouring water into a bucket with holes in it. No matter how much water you pour in, sooner or later it's going to run dry. Enjoy what God gives you, but aim higher than this world. Trust me, in the end you will be glad that you did.

"Strive to enter through the narrow gate..."

(Lk. 13:24)

RISK AGAIN...

"If there is no risk, then you will never accomplish anything great."

Our yard had a huge cottonwood tree when we were kids. My brothers and I were always climbing in it. The branches were strong, so we could climb pretty high in the tree. Once we reached a stopping point, we would slide out on a limb. The trick was to make sure you stopped before you reached the weak end of the branch. After all, it was a long way down if the limb snapped off. It was a risk, but exciting. However, it seems to me, that somewhere between childhood and early adulthood we stop taking risks, and when we do we halt our personal growth. If you want to make money, you have to risk losing it. If you desire a relationship with someone, you risk the chance of a broken heart. If you start your own business, you risk the chance of failure. If you choose to be a missionary, you risk losing your life in some foreign country. But remember - successful people take risks.

> *"...Be strong and of good courage; do not be afraid, nor be dismayed, for the Lord your God is with you wherever you go..."*
>
> *(Josh. 1:9)*

SPEND AGAIN...

"You can spend your life anyway you want, but you only get to do it once."

Who hasn't wished for "do overs?" Everyone has regrets about how they handled certain things in their lives. "If only," tends to be a phrase that flows from our mouths later in life. Once in a while we do get the chance to make amends, alter decisions, and have "do-overs", but not always. That's why it's so important to spend our time and our lives wisely. Steve Jobs once said, "If today were the last day of your life, would you want to do what you are about to do today?" If not, then don't do it. Spend your life creating the life you want. If you don't, you could end up using a lot of time cleaning up the life you never wanted. Before you know it, a huge portion of your life has passed you by, and you find yourself saying "if only" over and over again. Learn to use your remaining time on this earth wisely. You only get to spend it once.

> *"Now my days are swifter than a runner; They flee away...They pass by like swift ships..."*
>
> *(Job 9:25-26)*

RESIST AGAIN...

"The devil made me do it."

Personally, I believe that the only person who ever had a chance of getting away with that excuse was Eve. But she didn't and neither did Adam. God wouldn't accept it as a reason for their disobedience. He told them that they could eat from every tree in the garden except the tree of good and evil. But the temptation was just too much. They couldn't resist tasting the fruit on the forbidden tree and it cost them dearly. In fact, there's always a price to pay when we give in to temptation. Drink and drive and you could end up in jail. Pad your expense account and you could lose your job. Accept advances from the new guy or gal at the office, and you could end up divorced. "Free cheese," someone once said, "is always available in mouse traps." That's what falling into temptation does. It traps us, and the price we pay can be really high. We are bound to find ourselves in a tempting situation now and then. The best thing to do is pray for the Lord to give us the strength to resist, and simply walk away.

"Therefore submit to God. Resist the devil and he will flee from you."

(James 4:7)

WORSHIP AGAIN...

"Everyone worships something."

It's easy to start building our lives around something other than God. We have a goal in mind, something we want, and we become obsessed with reaching it. Now, there is nothing wrong with setting goals and obtaining them; everyone should do that. But often, the end result becomes the thing we worship. The business we built, the dream home, the sports car, our body, our bank account, etc. You begin to bow down to it day after day, working to maintain it. It becomes your "golden calf." Often, we are not even conscious of what we are doing. But all of the "false gods" that we worship can never satisfy our inner being. They cannot answer our prayers, sustain us during hard times, or carry us home to heaven. Only God can do that. Learn to worship Him first and to make Him your number one priority. When you do, everything else will fall into its proper place.

"You shall not make for yourself a
carved image...you shall not bow
down to them nor serve them."

(Ex. 20:4-5)

KNOW AGAIN...

"Learn to listen to your inner voice, it has more to say than you think it does."

God gave mankind a conscience, a built in warning system with an inner compass by which to gauge right and wrong. But the more we ignore that compass, the farther off course we get. Wrong becomes right as we begin to justify our behavior. After all, if I'm not hurting anyone, then what difference does my behavior make? But your behavior makes all the difference in the world. Why? Because when we sin, it offends God and separates us from Him. Keep sinning, and after a while God will simply give you over to the lifestyle you have chosen. God has no problem letting us have it our way. But remember, there's always a price to pay when we disobey the Lord. "For the wages of sin is death…" (Rom. 6:23). Read the Bible. Learn God's word and you will know what is "right" and what is "wrong."

> *"And even as they did not like to retain God in their knowledge, God gave them over to a debased mind, to do those things which are not fitting…"*

> *(Rom. 1:28)*

FIND AGAIN...

*"An honest assessment of oneself
can lead to personal growth."*

Children love to explore. To find new things, to see what's on the other side of the river, under the rock, up in the tree. Their curiosity pushes them on. As we grow older, we should never lose the desire to explore, especially our inner selves. Self-discovery helps us to answer questions about ourselves. Questions like: What do I believe? What do I want most out of life? What do I value most? What do I enjoy doing? Who do I like to spend my time with? What are my good qualities? My bad ones? What are my talents and gifts and where should I put them to work? What do I stand for or against? Self-discovery helps us to live a fuller life. It keeps us from being stagnant, helps us to grow, to reach for and expect more out of life. Life is a journey and we learn as we go. Uncover who it is you really are in your inner world by doing some soul searching.

*"And you shall know the truth, and
the truth shall make you free."*

(John 8:32)

FINISH AGAIN...

*"If the first half didn't go so well, adjust
your game plan for the second half."*

No matter how we started life, we can end stronger than we began. We can change direction, chart a new course and adjust our sails. We can leave this world with stronger faith, relationships, work ethic, giving, accomplishments, love and compassion. But in order to do that, we must never give up. We must push on; we must finish the race of life and never quit. Let's face it, life is hard and every day is a challenge to stay between the lines. Make adjustments and let go of what's not working. Try new paths and make new strategies. To be a winner in life, we have to finish solid, and to know that at the end of our lives we gave all we had to give. Forget about how you started and focus on finishing strong!

> *"I have fought the good fight, I have finished the race, I have kept the faith."*
>
> *(2 Tim. 4:7)*

LIVE AGAIN....

"There are no "do overs" when it comes to life."

Take your life one day at a time, and live it to its fullest. Don't dwell on the past or worry about the future. Learn to live in the present. Don't come to the end of your life full of regret, wishing you could do it all over again. Know why? You can't. This is it, so you better live it the way you want to now. The power is in your hands. You're the one that creates happiness or sadness, who loves or refuses to love, and who reaches out to others, or isolates yourself. Multiple opportunities come to each and every one of us every day of our lives. How we respond to them is entirely in our hands. So start every morning with the desire to get the most out of it, because this day will never ever come again. Live…and keep on living until the good Lord takes you home!

"…God is not the God of the dead, but of the living."

(Matt. 22:32)

ABOUT THE AUTHOR

Leanna has colored the lives of women for over twenty-five years by decorating, organizing, and merchandising their homes and businesses. Having walked with the Lord for more than forty years, five years ago, Leanna decided it was time to "decorate" the souls of women for the Lord. She began writing a newsletter called "Spiritual Revival", wrote a small book called, "The Color of Your Soul" and started "Color Your Soul" ministries. After taking a few years off for personal reasons, she recently revived her ministry. She holds numerous certifications in Women's Study's, Public Speaking, and a Bachelor Degree in Theology from Newburgh Seminary, along with a Creative Writing Degree. She is a native of Colorado, and has three children and two grandchildren.

www.ingramcontent.com/pod-product-compliance
Lightning Source LLC
Chambersburg PA
CBHW070816050426
42452CB00011B/2068